BRUTAL MINDS

The Beast C

H

Jamie Tarazi

Table of Contents

Dedication

I dedicate the whole book to my mum, who, despite experiencing high levels of mental adversity, managed to raise three boys into men but, more importantly, did this whilst dealing with historic life-changing issues which almost became life-ending. I couldn't comprehend how she managed to do it all. But she did, and in doing so taught me a lesson that shaped my life. That lesson was understanding.

Also one more thing I need you to know is that this book is based on my own experiences with mental health struggles. I don't expect everyone to take this book as some failsafe answer to improving mental health, I just hope you can take some positivity from my story.

About the Author

Jamie Tarazi is 48-years-old. He has a mum and two brothers, one older and one younger in his family, 40 years of a love-hate relationship with mental health, or being different as he likes to describe it ,has had a major impact on him. He has seen some of his closest family and friends broken by mental health whilst in himself trying to keep a strong positive mental attitude all the time. He has seen, experienced, and tried to solve one of the most sought after questions posed to people who have their own personal beasts, and that is *"Can I have a normal balanced life if I am afflicted with mental health issues with all its negative forms?"* He believes that the answer is yes, to a degree depending on how much people are willing to invest in the systems that he has been trying to create and hone for himself and others for the last 30 years.

Introduction

Mental health can affect everybody differently. I hope this book, if anything, can put into perspective my issues with mental health and how I try to deal with them.

I know that if you are affected by mental health issues, they can affect all life situations. I believe that my own issues with mental health have affected and promoted my attempts to develop a better way to deal with them.. With that in mind, whatever your affliction may be, even for those with no specific issues, you may be just interested in a system which helps to promote sustainable positivity, I hope you too can gain something from my book.

RESPONSIBILITY

I needed to write part of this book on single parenting because I believe the responsibility and the work involved in raising children, running homes and families is highly underrated and, if mental health issues are involved no matter how small, they need some form of understanding at a different level. This in no way lessens the mental health struggles from people who have no major responsibilities. Mental health really doesn't care either way, it will affect every susceptible person with equal negativity. I am solely coming from my own experiences and scenarios with my own personal, "beast." I feel this way because in certain environments mental health issues can become exponentially worse. Mental health issues become a lot harder to deal with on your own when you are laden with extra responsibilities, such as raising children and supporting households. If you are lucky enough to have a strong support system of family and friends this can help alleviate the shadow of mental health to some degree. I believe this shadow upon people with little or no support system can become very dangerous indeed. I can only write from the experience I had with my mum being on her own under her own personal shadows.

This book, I hope, will put into perspective the majorly important role positivity had to play in our family and how precious a gift my mum's teachings were. For anybody reading this book,"understanding" is the key.

One thing I feel I must point out is this: Nobody would choose to be afflicted by this beast called mental health, so I can only use my own experiences to try and help find solutions.

ME

I spent my whole childhood looking up to my mum. I think sometimes the person you become can be a direct result of what you absorb as a person from other people.So from a very young age for some reason, I had a very clear understanding of just what my mum actually did for us. The way that no matter how she felt, she still did the washing, still did the cleaning, still went to work, she spun so many plates to keep the home running so smoothly. She was under a lot of pressure, from being on her own as well as bringing up three boys.Looking back I think a lot of people would have struggled, but for some reason, my mum just kept on trucking, showed me the way, taught morals, ethics and an unswerving code of right and wrong. I experienced a lot of empathy and kindness as a child, and it became part of my personality.I learnt from an early age that consistent positivity is the key - not easy but......

TOO BUSY FOR MENTAL HEALTH

I have a section just for mums in general, with regards to mental health and the struggle they go through to become happy with themselves, both inside and out. It is very important for the readers to realise that my journey with mental health has been dramatically affected by the amount of responsibility I saw my mum take on whilst still working and running a fully functioning home with no external financial support. I believe a lot of women will be able to connect with what I am trying to explain about the standard amount of work women all over the world have to put in on a daily basis. And how sometimes your own issues become hidden and put away because of this workload. They put this work in because they have been given that responsibility from birth and before any thoughts of their own issues that may need dealing with become apparent, they have a family and a home to organise. A lot of men are in the same situation and have to bring a family up on their own; I think women are just expected to be domestic superheroes from birth. To everyone experiencing overwhelming responsibilities I hope you can connect with what I am trying to say. When the weight of responsibility that comes with trying to raise a family is put in the same arena as mental health, the weight can become too much. You may have many other responsibilities to deal with before your own issues and if those issues are based on mental health the weight from the beginning can be a heavy burden to carry. Hence, why I have the utmost respect and understanding for anybody with onerous responsibility who also has to maintain a positive mental attitude. All too often though, even with mental health being such a life changing affliction, you hide or swallow or just mask in general, the severity of your problems. As I reflect on this it seems to come across that I am only trying to reach out to single parents and women. I am not, so try not to judge me too harshly, I merely write from my own experiences. I just want anybody who has issues with mental health to maybe take something positive from the points I am trying to make.

Pieces of the Puzzle

There are many pieces of advice to my system, you will read them at different points throughout the book, please take even the smallest of these pieces of advice as seriously as the major ones because they all make up equally important pieces of my system for the self-manufacture of positive energy.

This statement "the self-manufacture of positive energy" is something I never thought possible for myself because when my mental health came for me, all I could really do was suffer until it left me of its own accord.

That is why part of the book is to include a section about wellbeing and nutrition. It's been a very important part of my self-production of positivity and also as part of the support system. The issues with high sugar and high cholesterol and other food related issues are well documented from a health and well-being stand point. How healthy eating helped me gain control of my weight issues and self-esteem and became one of the foundations of my system. I try to get natural vitamins and minerals through nutrition as opposed to pills and potions and the importance of learning all this information for yourself is invaluable.

I want the people who read the book to become self-sufficient. By this, I mean to use the system daily, to organise your own nutrition, and exercise to attain goals that you set for yourself. Thus, becoming your own vessel for the manufacture of positive energy. You can create many parts of your own positive support system; in effect, you are creating an armour for yourself to enable you to better deal with mental health issues.

With this book, I also want the readers who have no knowledge of mental health issues to understand how difficult the issues are.

From the overwhelming feeling of being out of control and panic-stricken to the almost unbearable sense of dread and sadness. I need to describe mental health this way because some of the readers may be the ones who take care of someone, or are just close to somebody with mental health issues, so it would be very informative for them to have an insight into the mind of someone like me, who has experience of mental health issues. I was asked in passing by one of my mates what I thought mental health was, because it had been on the news quite a lot, for me it is a feeling of dread,fear and panic whilst having a concrete duvet hanging over my head with my head being in a vice and that's just the physical part- so we'd better leave the mental side of my affliction well alone. There was a long silence, so I said I'm only joking how would I know, but it's probably very dark. You see how incredibly difficult it is to explain mental health without sounding theatrical, but it really does feel that way;

panic attacks, pressure headaches, self-doubt, and low self-esteem are just a few of the effects mental health has, and these can become daily occurrences if left alone to run rampant. You must never underestimate the strength of mental health's ability to destroy positivity; that's why creating a strong support system to deal with it is imperative. Mental Health and Children.

Mental health issues at a young age can really affect children. I believe we must empower our children with self-worth and confidence from an early age. It is important as parents that you take a vested interest in your child's mental well-being, ask questions, and gauge friendships so that you can get a picture of their state of mind.

The importance of support and positivity is major in children. What your children or child is surrounded by at a young age will have a serious effect on them when they get older. Use the system so that you may create for them a support system to help them with their own insecurities and fears, change their future, so the past can influence it positively. Whatever your issues are, they must not become your children's issues too.

Sometimes when somebody is affected by mental health it has the ability to affect their closest friends and family in a negative manner. Remember this, yesterday has to be dealt with yesterday not today and certainly not tomorrow.

Dwelling on past experiences in a negative manner is a recipe for disaster. You must always remember children have an amazing chance to be unaffected by mental health issues if they are treated like blank sheets of paper. Whatever you put on their particular clean sheet make sure as parents it is both positive and supportive. Children at a young age can have negative thoughts and feelings for various reasons, these reasons you may never even know about.It is just important to know that whatever the reason for the negative emotions; this could be just a part of their personality or their life surroundings, just try to communicate with your child accordingly. These little extra thought processes that you as an adult can bring to your child may just be the door they need to open to know you are there to support and understand if needed.Just to know somebody close to you understands is enough,sometimes not being asked about your well being can be an issue - if that's all you truly need. Children at a young age can be affected by your negative mental health problems.It's imperative that if you are affected, that you must try to put a system in place to deal with those negative emotions so that the possible effects on your family are lessened.

Chapter 1: The System of Understanding and Improving

Mental health needs to be treated as a significant social issue, I believe this because it has an effect on people's whole life. Education, employment, domestic situations, social surroundings all can be affected by mental health issues. If it is not adequately addressed it can affect all parts of life. It can also halt the production of positive energy by any individual.

I hope one of the reasons you bought the book was to try to understand and improve your personal situation or to understand better or improve someone else's with regards to mental health issues.

Now, as we go on this journey, know that I may use terminology that may seem strange to you, like using the term 'beast' when describing mental health. But, you must understand that I have seen with my own eyes how mental

health, and specifically depression and low self-esteem can destroy lives. So, I will apologise now if in some parts of this book it seems to sound like a Shakespearean play; but, you must realise the whole system I am trying to give to you is based on how my mind feels and deals with the daily, sometimes hourly, constant battle dealing with mental health.

The system I have created is based on two words, *understand* and *improve,* these two words cannot be taken lightly because they are the main foundation stones upon which the entire system is based upon. The system to which I am referring is a series of daily exercises and thought processes solely for the purpose of self-motivation and the self-production of positive energy with the opportunity to live a life that anybody with mental health issues can think is impossible. The goal for someone with mental health is really to live a life of normality. By normality, I mean an average of positive and negative feelings in something like equal measure, not predominantly negative, and also a set of normal reactions and thought processes to all manner of ordinary life situations that may crop up, from relationships to work, to recreation. Basically, to have a balanced and proportionate mixture of appropriate reactive emotions. You see, to a person with any form of mental health issues any negativity within basic life scenarios can bring life-changing or life-ending results. Every time there is negativity in any of these areas, there is a chance for some people that it may escalate into something more sinister.

The whole point of my entire system is to get you to a place where you can actually deal with situations and not let them automatically send you to a negative place, but to take control of them in an orderly, positive manner. My whole system is about the manufacture of positive energy, so you can be in control and understand the negative mental feelings when they start to occur for whatever reasons.

SHATTERED

I once likened mental health to a broken mirror, lots of fragments, some positive and most negative, both having the ability to cut, the broken shards of the mirror being consistently inconsistent. This makes it almost impossible to put back together. It is that set of unequal predominantly negative emotions that makes it difficult for people to deal with their own mental health issues. The reason I say both positive and negative emotions cut is that for some reason when we are in a situation that we feel is not positive, we will sort through the positive shards of the mirror to find the negative shards which usually find a way to blame ourselves for whatever negative situation we find ourselves in.When these negative situations arise, instead of thinking of a solution to the problem and designing a plan to sort out that particular issue, we dwell on the actual negativity arising from the negative situation we find ourselves in, and that seems to be what we become engulfed in and that becomes the place we stay.

My system simply requires that we give a certain percentage of emotions for varying life situations, by this I mean that instead of cutting all your fingers sorting through

11

endless piles of broken mirror to find those all-important negative "I'm the issue" shards of mirror, you may just find the strength to designate the correct amount of appropriate 'I'm actually a good person emotion' to apply to any life scenario you may encounter just remember it's not always your fault. Always remember mental health doesn't care how you feel; it will always bring negativity. You must care how you feel and bring positivity.

Anyone with mental health issues may find decision making in certain situations quite hard. This is because I believe it creates many "what if scenarios" and with this creates a consistently inconsistent mindset. The main problem here is you find it incredibly difficult to make decisions and stick to them without overthinking them. The main focus of my system is to flip this and for you to become positively consistent. This is very important because as a person who is affected by mental health issues may not have the ability to make life choices based on common sense and normality. Sometimes, their decisions are more impulsive . I think people with mental health issues are in a constant state of overthinking and mental anguish quite similar in effect to the broken mirror when some decisions are to be made. I mean that there are too many conflicting emotions in your mind at the same time when you may need a consistent chain of standard thought processes when decision making is required. To some extent the choices you have are too varied and too much in number to make an easy decision. Sometimes consistent thought and decision making, if learned, can be of great benefit. Situations can be categorised and dealt with in a much more logical and standard way, what comes after certain situations is usually a large number of second guessing and regret. You see,the issue isn't the situation because situations are always going to be fluid yet constant.It's about what I have to do to deal with making these choices in these situations. So let's say I have an argument with my wife, the argument I can have quite easily, that isn't the issue, the issue is what comes afterwards. Whereas my wife quite normally would think nothing of it. We've been together 22 years so it's just an argument. I can tell you right now that not minutes after the argument I would be second guessing and questioning my decisions. I would have to seriously take steps from my own system to get into my head that it was just an argument and my wife isn't going off with another man and she probably won't divorce me because I ate all the pasta and my son will have to have noodles for tea. It sounds crazy but what most people would call trivial can become disproportionate. Low self-esteem and confidence play massive roles here because of the constant part they play in the cycle of mental health issues

The thought of just making a decision based upon rationality and what you see before you seems to be an almost impossible task. I believe this is due to negative thought processes that seem to become an inherent part of a person afflicted with mental health issues. Simply put, I call it an action-reaction. When you think about the reaction to your action, and it then changes your action, when really you should have enough confidence in yourself to be able to carry them out without permanently second guessing yourself. You need to stop thinking about the reaction to that action in such detail because that in itself changes how you deal with certain situations and decision making. I hope my book can bring you to a point where you can just make decisions without doubt and self-questioning being defining factors in your making of decisions. We must all look toward a life where we make decisions based on our own confidence in our own character and person. Know this, if you are a good person in life and try your best at everything you do, then it is an amazing personality trait, and you must never forget that. If you base your decision making on your own core values, they will always be positive and true. You must learn to back yourself and have confidence in yourself. If you can do this, it will, in some part, go towards you having an understanding of your mental health issues and not having other people play such a major role in your decision making.

I try to live my life by one simple rule: what's right is right and what's wrong is wrong and I try to have the confidence of my conviction. Simply put, I try not to justify to myself the reasons for my actions.

You may find that mental health may be with you all the time, but mental health does not define who you are, you define who you are.

And again...

YOU DEFINE WHO YOU ARE!

If anything, your mental health must remind you of who you truly are and what you are capable of. If not dealt with at the right time, being different can stop you from being the person you are meant to be.

I invented an exercise to help me when I feel my negative beast of mental health is coming for me. I call it, *THE MIRROR.*

When I start to feel anxious, depressed, or anything associated with negativity, I try to do the direct opposite of what my mind is trying to make me do. It's quite amazing that in some of my darkest times I found myself having the best weight training sessions, some of the best adventures with my son, and some very emotional times with my wife. You see, for me, I could never understand why negativity seemed to be so much more of a powerful emotion than positivity.

Then I realised that the journey to become truly happy and positive is just that. 'a journey'. It takes consistent work every day for you to realise your potential for creating positivity. You must never forget it's no good trying to fight the beast without an appropriate weapon and that weapon is the realisation of your own self-worth.

You may be wondering why this particular book on mental health is any different to the thousands of others out there, and what makes me qualified to write about a subject that is surrounded by so much confusion and mystery so freely? Well, I hope to show you an insight into mental health from a unique point of view. You see, I have not only experienced mental health from my own battles but also from being surrounded by it and having it negatively affect my loved ones.

I have spent a lifetime trying to find a strategy to deal with and have a life with mental health. My life journey has always been under the glare of mental health, because in some ways when you have lived with this beast perched upon your shoulder it will be a constant in your life forever. If it is not directly affecting your life on a day-to-day basis, it seems to just sit on your shoulder, waiting to engulf you again with the ever-present heavy mental cloud that not only covers and blinds you but also fills you with sheer dread as the weight continues to crush you, (this is one of my descriptions of my own mental health).This is why the majority of the people I have met with mental health issues can, at best, ride out these familiar storms, waiting for a break in the black clouds to give a bit of respite and hope. Yet, again, the tempest has passed for now with hopefully as much damage limitation as possible.

It may seem quite strange to some people the way I describe mental health, but all I am doing is trying to describe to you how I feel and how I have had mental health issues related to me. I hope you will make a connection of sorts in some part because, however over the top, my descriptions may sound to you that there is a real fear and dread felt by a lot of people with mental health issues. Whatever the main emotion attached to your mental state is, without being a mind reader, I can guarantee it is predominantly negative. This, in turn, has an overall jaded way in which you live your life waiting for the inevitable beast to return. Mental health issues have a way about them that makes you second guess yourself in a lot of situations. This could revolve mainly around your low self-esteem issues and confidence issues.

Now, as I mentioned, certain emotions such as low *self-esteem* and *confidence*, are quite prevalent within mental health. When we have healthy normal levels of self-esteem and confidence, we feel positive about ourselves and our life as well. Low self-esteem and confidence can in a lot of cases, as I said before, begin in childhood. Whatever surrounds us as children and the situations we encounter can drastically affect our lives. This is amplified, I believe, if you are prone for whatever reason towards low self-esteem or confidence and then can have catastrophic implications later on in life. Any negativity that implies that we are not good enough stays with us within our subconscious. This is incredibly difficult to fix but I believe my system can alleviate some of this negativity at least. Perhaps you find it difficult to live up to other people's expectations or your own. If you have low self-esteem or confidence, you may hide yourself from social interaction, do not try new things, and avoid things that you find challenging. It makes you stay in a bubble and does not let you grow into the person you could be.

It's pretty amazing how little you can think of yourself when you do not particularly respect or like yourself, to start with. You find yourself in a life situation where you put pressure upon yourself to be something you are not. By this, I mean for some reason, mental health issues turn a lot of people into a servant caste which, I believe, is solely down to the lack of self-esteem and respect you have for yourself and your almost need for people, however manipulative or

18

negative, to love and appreciate you. The most basic yet complex lesson to learn is to interact and surround yourself with positive, caring, and trustworthy people, people in effect, that are just like you.One major bonus of attaining this is that you will have a positive environment, both socially and in work, from which you can start to feel positive and confident in yourself. If you can build a positive family base with a partner who respects you and will always have your back, this is the strong foundation from which you can start to put your positive mental health system into action.

To get healthy self-esteem, you need to identify negative beliefs that you have about yourself and then challenge them. I know it is not an easy task. It will take a lot of time, and you must be patient. It is a slow process, of course you must not expect instant results. It will take a long time, and if you want it to work in the long run, you have to realise consistency over time is the only way forward. Otherwise, it will only ever be temporary. You might have low self-confidence for very justifiable reasons, like, if something happened in your childhood while growing up. For whatever reasons there are solutions for it. It entirely depends on the person who is suffering as to how much they want to grow and develop their life into a positive one. "You must try to love and respect your reflection in the mirror."

We all have a part in our lives where we encounter difficult and challenging times, these can usually mould you as a person to some degree; it's quite dangerous if you dwell only on the negative, it will inevitably affect you negatively today and tomorrow. You have to sometimes; if you can remember that something happened for a reason that was out of your control, you need to stop blaming yourself. Forget yesterday, it's about going forward today and tomorrow with a positive mindset.

You may sometimes find yourself in a situation where you are worried about a friend, family member, or colleague. You must try to find ways to support them. In my opinion, the best thing you can do for someone is to try to understand them. For this, you need to become very familiar with empathy. You need to try and understand what your friend or loved one is feeling. If you don't know what they are feeling, the first step is to talk. If you wait for that person to come to you for help, it will probably never happen because mental health amongst the other afflictions it brings also brings an overwhelming set of thought processes that make you extremely introverted. If you keep knocking on that door, they may just answer. I became almost embarrassed and closed in mentally. You end up almost storing all the negative energy up until the point of another mirror breaking. If you can spot situations like these occurring you might be able to find out what is troubling them and have some knowledge on what you can do to help them. Silence, irritability, sudden changes in character may be signs that your loved one or friend maybe needs a chat, just try it you'll soon know if they do or don't and can address it accordingly.

Now I cannot claim to know all the facets of mental health; that would be near impossible, as the different shades of mental health are too numerous to possibly think of having specific systems to combat each one separately. The system I put together is based on my personal experiences in trying to deal with my personal beast and the people close to me with similar afflictions. This system may seem quite complex with many parts and many daily checkpoints (we will discuss checkpoints later). But in reality, I have just tried to put together a template that can not only be used for people with mental health issues but also for the people who maybe would like the knowledge, so if needed could help and understand anyone they are connected to get through any negative mental health issues they might encounter. I just want to make the reader understand and benefit from a system of self-manufactured positive energy.

This system, as well as helping people with mental health issues, can equally be used by people with none, to understand and improve daily life and goal-reaching by the simple premise of self-motivation and the manufacture of your own positive energy.

I hope this book, to some degree, may bring an understanding and appreciation for the pain, both; mental and physical, that this horrific condition brings.

My system, at its core, if you are to reap the maximum benefits, relies solely on how much you want to put into it. By this, I mean your need not to be ruled by the beast, but how much you need to live a more consistent positive life. You may say that I have positivity in my life, yet I am still ruled by mental health issues. I believe this is because self-manufacturing enough positive energy as you require is essential and forms another foundation in my system.

The continuing manufacture of positive energy consistently.

Another thing I want you to know is that this book on mental health may be a little disjointed in parts, but I hope you understand that I am trying to write this book with mental health issues. I think that with my small interjections of mental health information and positive actions that you will be able to connect and build from what I have written to help you or someone close to you understand and deal with some of the many issues associated with mental health.

Chapter 2: Understanding the 'Beast'

So, the first problem we will tackle is to the people with no issues at all. This one is for the husbands, wives, boyfriends, girlfriends, or just friends of people with issues. It must be very frustrating trying to sort out something they cannot see, understand, or experience. Just trying to keep normality within families and relationships can be near impossible when a loved one or friend has this affliction. The one thing you have to get your head around is unconditional understanding. This term actually has to work both ways, from whoever has the issues to whoever does not. Imagine, if you can, a situation where somebody's emotions can swing from positive to negative at the drop of a hat. This, in turn, can end up in all manner of altercations and arguments.

Now, imagine this person is someone you love or just care for, and these altercations and arguments are quite regular in number. At some point, you will think to yourself: 'is this ever going to end?' At what point do you say, 'enough is enough'. Well, in short you will not, because a lot of mental health issues will always be part of a personality. What needs to be known is this: mental health is to be understood and dealt with accordingly if it is to keep the person affected in a state of control and consistency. This is because usually, mental health issues have the trait of making you feel totally out of control and overwhelmed. You

23

must learn the ability to spot the same red flags, and by this, I mean the same things that set off anxieties and issues every time; it could be stress, money, families, relationships or just the constant pressure of trying to live with mental health. All of these red flags need to be dealt with in the same way, and that's where unconditional understanding steps in.

PERCENTAGES

Imagine that mental health is like one drop of black ink in a pint of clear water, the tiny amount of black ink would discolour the whole pint of clear water so imagine how many drops of clear water it would take to turn a pint of black ink clear. My point is only this, mental health can make even the most positive situation negative at the drop of a hat. That's why it is so important to arm yourself with a system that has the ability for you to produce positivity on a regular basis. Mental health can bleed into every facet of life. This is because mental health is like having a perpetual portion of black ink always ready to discolour your pint of fresh clear positive water.

This could come from all manner of standard situations; a small argument of no particular significance can quickly turn explosive if the mental health issues are not taken into consideration. If you are the person dealing with someone with mental health issues, it's very important you understand these potential flashpoints.

I have often thought that the understanding and acceptance of mental health can be likened to trying to learn right from wrong. There are basically two ways you can go about this: you can take the approach of when someone has done something negative you can have an argument based upon the fact they have done something negative, or have a conversation as to why they felt they had to do something negative, these two approaches can have vastly different outcomes. What I mean by this is whenever you get into a negative situation with mental health, let's say your partner is depressed and down in the dumps, and starts to create arguments for no or little reason, instead of reacting to that specific negative action you must try to think deeper about why this person is doing these negative things, once you start to treat mental health from this point of view you start to see it in a different light. Mental health can be lived with if you realise that first, you must understand the beast in order to really start to live a life with it. From the point of view of a person with this affliction, you must understand that if you do not deal with the cause of mental health and not just the effect, you will get into a very negative cycle of just trying to deal with mental health when it affects you. You really need to know why it is affecting you and have a consistent plan to deal with it when it comes. Finding the cause of mental health issues can be a lot harder than you think. Every mental health issue can have a separate link to a specific act or issue that that person has experienced in their life. So finding the cause of specific issues can be like finding a needle in a haystack as it relies heavily on the affected person being confident enough to either share this with you or even confident enough for them to come to terms with it themselves.

Because mental health has this innate ability to make you think it's all your fault anyway, disregarding the circumstances of any scenarios that could have caused your mental health issues, it becomes increasingly difficult to understand and put into perspective in a consistent fashion your own personal mental health issues. I believe in a lot of cases, if you can start the process of not blaming yourself permanently and with the positive energy manufactured from my system, it's a great beginning to self-healing.

LEARN FROM THE CHILDREN

Knowledge is power, and as you know, young children do not intentionally want to hurt or harm you; they just act a certain way because they live in the moment.This is the deciding factor in how they deal with certain situations, and usually, it is up to you as an adult to take this into consideration when dealing with situations.

For all intents and purposes, you may think that it's just about agreeing and bowing down when a situation rears its head, but there is far more to it than that. If you try to, for a minute, just understand what is going on within the mindset of the person who is affected by mental health and understand that rational thinking does not apply here, you can start to put into place a system to deal with negative

situations when they occur,

I was told once by a man I respected and loved that to experience severe mental health issues was likened to a blanket of heavy dread being wrapped around your head. It was described to me in such a frightening fashion that I actually thought he was experiencing the feeling at the time. When he was telling me about it, he spoke of it as if it was an actual physical presence, and that he could feel massive pressure upon his skull, almost drowning in quicksand, was the impression he gave me of his personal experience of it.

Now, if I had not experienced mental health issues at that level, I may have thought that he was just over exaggerating his feelings, but I know it is incredibly difficult to cope with something that, at best, is just about bearable yet, at worst, life-changing and sometimes life-ending. The root cause of mental health issues can be caused by many experiences that you might have. Physical, sexual, financial, or any kind of negative experience in your life may have the ability to set off serious mental health issues. That is why it is critically important that this root cause is realised and understood, and dealt with at an early point.

You must remember a person with mental health issues walks a very fine line when your day is good, you will be thankful when your day is bad you can become miserable incredibly quickly. This has a lot to do with how certain life situations pan out for you if you had, let's say: low self-esteem issues prior to a certain situation occurring; what happens in some cases is that an already bad situation evolves into an almost unliveable one. So, all of a sudden, to somebody with mental health issues, who finds most days mentally taxing anyway, one standard bad situation occurs, like maybe you cannot afford petrol for your car or food shopping or an altercation at work or with a partner, can if left alone make an already cracked mirror shatter. And by shatter, I mean a possible life-ending or life-changing set of thoughts. I believe everything is linked when it comes to the effects of mental health issues. Linking issues in the mind of somebody who has mental struggles is devastating, so suddenly not having enough money for petrol on its own maybe isn't an issue, but if you link this with maybe a relationship issue and a work issue and an already overwhelming feeling of low self-esteem can, when linked together become the mountain that cannot be climbed. If you had a coping system in place to counteract the negative link syndrome, maybe you wouldn't be inclined to link all these negative thoughts together and create such a dangerous situation. All negative scenarios in life must be dealt with a consistent mindset, and we must plan to overcome them separately. We must try to get away from the linking mentality where you can sometimes make a really big negative picture from separate negative situations.

Another factor in all this is not just bad situations causing mental health issues, but also it could be a chemical imbalance or any other medical reason for mental health issues. It does not always come from a dark past and horrific experiences. It can actually be the fact that your brain does not produce a certain chemical in the quantity required to live a normal life, the bonus if you can call it that is that it may be able to be controlled to a degree by medication and also the knowledge that it is a medical issue, to know that your mental health is purely a medical issue is in itself a really big deal.

The fact that you have to deal with past issues which are the root of your mental health can be a lot more challenging So, imagine a person who has self-confidence issues and also has low self-esteem issues to start with, add to that a life-changing set of negative experiences, that just loads extra mental weight onto an already fractured mind. Compounded by a lack of certain chemicals within the brain specifically manufactured to deal with certain emotions, You can see how a lot of issues that on their own could be dealt with. It's when they become linked together negatively that they become a whole lot more dangerous. You would be surprised how many people cannot empathise with the severity of these situations. This is why sometimes if somebody is trying to understand mental health, they must take all these different mental facets into consideration when dealing with a friend, family member or partner with issues.

If anything, these issues are pretty standard within the mental health community. That's why I think sometimes it is easier to get to grips with the medical side of mental health rather than the emotional side. I mean that if issues are purely medical, a support system in place to directly assist your problems in the form of doctors and a medical framework of organising the problem from a purely logical standpoint. Yet somehow, when the core issue is emotional, which has to be dealt with both medically and emotionally, for whatever reason, it seems incredibly difficult to treat. In part, this is so because no matter how much medication or counselling, if the person who has the mental health issues cannot deal with or live with their own personal beasts, then the process becomes increasingly difficult to manage. Being able to live and prosper with yourself is a majorly important piece of the puzzle. When you become happy with the person you are, you can then start to become the person you want to be. Getting to this point will vary hugely from person to person. Many things must be in place before the feeling of positive self-worth to be attained; counselling and time are just a couple of things that can help in this particular part of mental health. The complex thought processes and emotions of the mind are almost impossible to comprehend and thus are increasingly difficult to find a solution for .All I will say is this the answer, in my opinion, is within the person. Only they know the answer, and eventually, through a long process of understanding and communication and positivity will you start to see the small glimmers of light, add to this the ability to maybe produce your own positive energy consistently it may just be the piece of the puzzle that has been missing.

This following set of exercises and mental mantras are the systems I have used to not only control my mental health issues but to actually better my life living with them. So, before you start on your own personal journey, remember that the system only works with consistency. You must be consistent in every facet of this system for it to work. It may seem to you minuscule and insignificant but believe me, I followed the system to the letter, and it does work if you let it. All manner of different people can benefit from this system simply because what the system requires of you is tiny in comparison with what the system gives you in the long term, but like I said before, it all depends on the level of consistency you are willing to give. And remember you can tailor all facets of this system to your own levels. Remember it's the completion of goals that brings happiness, the goals don't have to be huge or massive in number.

REMEMBER, CONSISTENCY IS

THE KEY.

Chapter 3: Penny and a Push-Up

In a world of social media and crazy levels of vanity the hustle and speed of life can make your mental health a legit beast. Try to maintain a consistent average of emotions by regular active routines to keep our minds in a positive place. Adopting these exercises may reduce your anxiety, depression, and negativity and could result in improving your self-esteem as well as cognitive functions.

For this, I have specifically designed a series of activities that really helped me during my struggling times. I want to share it with anyone who is suffering from any kind of mental health illness and hope that if anything it may give you the same semblance of normality and consistency it gave me. If you know of someone who may be suffering with mental health problems these systems may in some way alleviate some of the weight mental health brings Nutrition is one of the most important pillars in regard to mental stability, I never underestimated this because for me when I disliked myself, I hurt myself, enter the 'whatever' mindset which basically means whatever was bad for me I ate. Now some people might drink, smoke, take drugs whatever it is you use to justify how bad you feel, you do it to excess.

Now let's say you have an addictive personality; this can turn this situation into a very dangerous one. Now just imagine if you could use that addictive trait in a positive way to improve your life and wellbeing. Nutrition has always been linked to health and wellbeing ,but rarely has it been put in simple terms because the relationship between your mind and your body is extremely intricate and also to add the effect of nutrition upon these two entities, is also extremely complex. You must understand that I worked out a long time ago that if you do not treat your body like a solid relationship with give and take in equal measure the price you can pay would be extremely negative. The release of chemicals from the brain and body in response to certain situations you put your body into with regards to nutrition and stress can greatly affect mental health. I will go into this in further detail later on in the book but for now let us embark on a journey that will hopefully not only bring you positivity in the short term, but give you the ability to manufacture positive energy in the long term. As one of the main principles of my system, I firmly believe that the state of your physical self has a massive effect on your mental health.

Welcome to Brutal Mindset.

Penny and a Push-Up – Week One:

This system will only work if you give hundred percent consistency. I needed something to change, this allowed Changes happen to me. I hope it does the same for you.

Now, what I want you to do is, get a plastic cup, a pen, and an empty diary would be perfect, but a paper pad will do. Put them on the floor and keep the cup in your line of sight, one foot away from your head. Do this so there is no chance of any collision with the cup and any part of your body.

Now breathe in through the nose, out through the mouth, empty your mind, think of the last time you laughed so much it hurt and think of this for at least ten seconds.

Now get into the press up position and complete one press up, nice and slow, chest to floor with good technique and put one penny in the jar. If you cannot do a press up, do one on your knees. I do press-ups, but any bodyweight exercise will do; an air squat, or sit up. Just remember to keep good technique with any exercises you do and make sure that the exercises are within your capabilities. Make sure to keep your cup in full view at all times.

When you are done with the exercise and have put the penny in the plastic cup, I want you to clear your mind and breathe deeply both in and out; four or five counts will do. Just think to yourself, nobody can take that press-up from me, and nobody can take that penny. Think to yourself: I have just improved my life, financially and physically, and I am totally in control of those two actions, in this minute, I decide the outcome. What you must remember is this, the fact that it is just a penny and just one press up has no consequence at this point on your mindset, try not to think of

35

the amount of money however insignificant you may think it is and just think of the consistency you are trying to gain from the system itself. Also you may think that the amount of physical work needed to do one press up is also insignificant well don't forget at the beginning of this journey all you are trying to understand and put into practice is consistent positive actions so it's not the amount or how hard it is that is the key it's the fact that you are doing it consistently that counts.

Daily Life Diary

Next, write down in your diary a time in your life when you were most proud of something you have achieved. It could be qualifications, children, savings; it just must be specific here; a time, a place, the reason. All equally important, above all it must be something that has stayed in your mind and brings you positive, proud memories and write it down next to number one.

Now you may find yourself struggling to pull these positive achievements from your life but it is so incredibly important that you do. Sometimes mental health makes you believe you have no valid achievements. Believe me, you have. This could be the first time you sit down with your loved ones and chronicle your positive life achievements. Now, that is the first day of your journey complete and the first workout done. You may be thinking, "Well, what was the point of all that? I have saved a penny and done one push up and found it incredibly difficult to write something positive about myself.

The Reason

This next part is what I really need you to remember, if you can place in your mind this mantra, "what I have just achieved is much less than I know myself to be capable of" then we are already in the early stages of positive mental energy. If you can always think you can do more, that in itself puts you in a position of control because you have completed the goal, yet you know you can do more. At this moment you are in a state of wanting to do more and envisaging doing more. All these emotions are linked with self-improvement,goal attainment and positivity. These are the positive links you need to start connecting together to improve your mental and physical state.

Repeat these actions seven times to complete an entire week. So at the end of the week, you will have accomplished seven reps of your chosen exercise, you will have seven pennies or pounds in your plastic cup and you will have seven proud life moments listed in the start of your life diary.

When you get up in the morning to do your penny and push up routine you must read the past days' proud moments from your life diary and try to remember them for at least five minutes and if you can try to smile for about ten seconds at least before you begin the workout. I would suggest you do this system in the early morning; if possible, 5:30-6:00 am would be perfect. Get used to getting up at this time and finish with a shower. It's well-documented that early exercise and positive mindsets work hand in hand as a very important part of this whole system.

The whole system you are undertaking is based on an idea I had some years ago that I named minimal consistency. This, in a nutshell, is the completion of minuscule physical and mental exercises to release certain chemicals from your brain and body. I have always been fascinated by the way in which my mental health affects me so trying to map my mental health's high and low points became of optimum importance. I often wondered why some days I would be in a good positive place yet other days I would be in a bad negative place when there was no change in my personal situation. So I started really looking into what the brain does regarding our memories and emotions. What I found was that the brain and body releases certain chemicals in certain situations in certain amounts and that there are literally hundreds of variables when we link this brain to emotional connection. I will go into this in further detail later on in the book as it sits well with my health and nutrition section later on.

When you are affected by mental health issues, you tend to forget self-worth and achievement, welcoming negativity as the norm. We too easily fall into the trap of feeling that we are the issue. In reality, you need to realise your own self-worth to see that you can deal with negative situations in life in a more balanced and understanding way. You must become consistent in your thoughts and actions when tackling negative life situations. That is why applying the daily system of reinforcing your self-worth by remembering your most positive achievements in life through the life diary is essential. The physical portion of the system is so incrementally small at the beginning that anyone can apply it, although as the months and years go on the physical side of the system will get increasingly tougher. This revolves around the fact that although at the beginning you may feel the physical part of the system is easy, fast forward one year, and depending on how hard you push yourself; the one press up could easily be twenty or even thirty; at this stage, you will realise why the increments had to be so small at the beginning. The ability to go from one to thirty press-ups but having the controlled consistency to do it over a long passage of time will only amplify the fact that any goal in life that to you means something like better mental health, weight loss, financial, anything that isn't going to be quick to make it truly worth the journey.

The same applies to the pennies I use. Pennies not for any other reason than to show you control the amount and the number it could easily be pound and a push up or so on and so forth it's all under your control.

Now whilst doing the exercises you may start to feel a little pump in your chest or your arms or anywhere in your body. This is a direct result of you doing small amounts of exercise. Just think that you are getting stronger and healthier for minimal input. Look at the cup and read the life diary, and realise this is the start of my journey. All I have to do is learn consistency, and it will all fall into place. Do not underestimate the power of consistency – just remember that everything you are doing, from positive thoughts to cups with pennies or pounds in them to repetitions of exercises, you only reap the rewards if they are consistently accomplished on a daily basis. Thus, the self-manufacture of that vital positive energy is needed to keep the beast at bay.

You will soon realise that all the exercises and pennies become addictive. I need to carry on with my penny and push up because all the work and results I have got from my system are too precious to me to give up .

Penny and a Push-Up – Week Two:

Now, to further continue with the mindful activity: put two pennies in your cup and do two push-ups, and write in your diary one personal positive act you have done in your life. It could be helping somebody or any action that reflects your heart and the person you are. The only stipulation is that it must be positive. This, again, needs to be completed for a full week. You may feel these actions are so small that they cannot benefit you, but once again these actions are part of a much bigger plan that depends on you consistently accomplishing these small goals. Once again you may need your close friends and family to assist you in compiling these positive life diary entries.

'Goals' are also an interesting part of the system. Goals, for most people, are quite simple to achieve, but when it comes to mental health, they become an altogether different animal. With mental health, it seems that just living your life is hard enough. To most, setting and accomplishing goals is a dream that simply cannot be realised. That is why my system relies on incredibly small goals. So when you have achieved the relatively small physical and mental goals within the system, you may start to do the same in your life in general So, for me, it might be that the next time my son irritates me, I will stop and think before I react, and I will ask myself: Why is he acting like that? And what considerations must I understand before I will make any snap judgements? There are regrets we may feel from flying off the handle too quickly or making snap judgements that can result in negativity which, as we know, is what we are trying to avoid.

The consistency in your positive thought processes like thinking "Why is somebody acting a certain way, before I act a certain way" is reinforced by the consistency you show in the penny and the push up. This helps in both the understanding of mental health and the explanation of mental health. I believe also that this process strengthens your consistent mindset as well. I hope that alongside the mainly mental health oriented theme my book is going down that everybody without any issues can also benefit from the ways I am trying to teach. I truly believe that at its core this system of trying to produce consistent positive mental energy can benefit both the affected and unaffected.If these understanding principles are integrated into your life, you will benefit.

Penny and a Push-Up – Week Three:

This time, we will do three push-ups and put three pennies in our cup. At this point, you must now start to gauge your fitness levels. You may have to stay on one push up for quite some time, that's fine just make sure the pennies go up at the normal rate and the press ups will come in time. This time when you open your life diary, I want you to write down your aspirations, important goals you would like to accomplish in your life one through seven as before

Random thought for the day..

One of my worst traits is regret.

42

Regret is a very damaging emotion in the sense that unless you have a system in place to deal with it effectively it can have seriously negative effects on your state of mind and is a breeding ground for self-doubt and various mental health issues.

If you get into a cycle where you seem to be reflecting on your past decisions and situations with regret and negativity, it is necessary to have what I call an anchor. By this, I mean a life diary of achievements and goals and all the positive things you have done in your life to counteract the negative regret and guilt that you can sometimes become surrounded by.

What is a full life diary

A full life diary is very different from the weekly life diary that accompanies you through the brutal mindset system; this is because the full life diary will take a long time to compose. It must have within its pages every positive and happy time you have experienced or as many as you can remember in your entire life also, all of your achievements play a huge role in your full life diary as they are a reflection of the true person you are. You can forget too soon your achievements, and especially for those with mental health issues remembering these achievements is of paramount importance.

I had to realise a long time ago that although I felt a lot of regret and guilt about parts of my life, when I thought about it clearly much was down to external factors. I often think that maybe back then, if I would have had my own personal positive life diary to draw on, things may have been different for me. I know one thing: I would've appreciated the person in the mirror a bit more.

Penny and a Push-Up – Week Four:

Four pennies, four push-ups, one last list. Now this list is very important because this list is a list of what you think maybe stopping you attaining your goals and what you need to do to attain your goals: so it may be fitness, confidence, self-esteem, finance whatever it is write them down and always remember you can't go back in time, but what you can do is orchestrate a series of goals which will help ensure that the same mistakes and thoughts are not repeated.

Now when the first month is over, you will probably be in the middle of sorting lists, trying to make sense of your particular journey, and this is when groundhog day will start; my whole system requires you to do is the same thing over and over again – put your pennies or pounds in the jar do your chosen exercise and try to attain the small goals you set yourself.

Keeping a life diary with you at all times is essential. You must constantly be able, at times of stress, to physically see your achievements and goals. You may add things as you go on such as a healthier diet, gaining extra qualifications in whatever your chosen field is, whatever really, as long as it is a goal that you feel would benefit you if you complete it.

The exercises will obviously have to be tailored to your level of fitness, but the idea is really that eventually, over time, you will become fitter, faster, healthier, and maybe a bit richer, but definitely more confident within yourself from your achievements. So let's recap. You have had a month of physical and mental tasks. What happens next is this: as the weeks go by you will consistently hopefully increase your chosen exercise and increase your penny or pound container. The amount of improvement both financially and physically is entirely in your control. Just remember that whatever numbers you put to your pennies and pushups must stay consistent for at least seven days. If at any point you need to reduce either pennies or push ups do so with the same consistency. Because life is also a number of ups and downs and positive and negative. Your particular journey will at times reflect this. Just remember if you try to stay consistent you will always have something to be extremely proud of. Because however small the percentage of positive energy it takes to get up in the morning and do something that benefits you, that positive energy will become the catalyst for your own ability to produce positive energy. This ability to maybe feel positive from within yourself, by yourself could be a very important tool to anybody trying to improve their health. Both mentally and physically.

I will now set up for you my brutal mindset system. I will set this up as before, with a full month of the system to show you how yours might look.

WEEK ONE MONDAY

6.00 am (tired)

1. Set up my workout space, placed a plastic cup within view, and put my empty diary with a pen next to it. Place one pound in my cup and get into a push-up position, clear my mind and do one push-up nice and slow. Now I take several deep breaths and concentrate on clearing my mind, now I think to myself, one push up, one pound. I know I can do more but I know also I must follow the system fully and to the letter to get all the benefits. The next thing is my life diary so for week one, every day I must write something . today's proud point is when I won a cup playing rugby it felt amazing and when I remember back to those days it makes me smile with all the positivity surrounding me playing rugby and great friends. This also makes me feel a great feeling of achievement because team sports, in general, are based on friendships, positivity, and journeys. I advise anybody to become part of a team in any sport, from rugby to tabletop

miniature gaming, as it is a great way to surround yourself with people like yourself.

Next, I grab a shower and start my breakfast.

Note to self: Getting up early and doing physical exercises makes me feel good. Next breakfast.

BREAKFAST

100g breakfast oats (good source of carbs provides antioxidants and lowers blood sugar amongst other benefits) with enough water or milk to create a desired consistency. I use almond milk (high in vitamin e, which is good for lowering the risk of strokes and heart disease) and cook in the microwave to your own personal temperature. Then, when cooked, I add two tablespoons of blueberries and two tablespoons of chopped strawberries (good sources of vitamin C, good for bones, teeth, and general good functioning of the immune system), then I add one tablespoon of Greek yogurt (high protein, low fat and very rich in probiotics for good gut health) then to finish a teaspoon of honey (because it's nice) I also have a pint of water with super greens powder for extra vitamins and minerals.

Now, this breakfast is absolutely your own choice; this is just mine, but for me to buy into my own system, I had to back it up with good nutrition, but the choice is yours.

WEEK ONE TUESDAY

6.00 am (tired)

Set up your workspace and place the cup in the same position. I have a weird feeling of accomplishment when I hear the sound of yesterday's pound coin in my cup as I add today's interesting thing. Next, I get into a press-up position, clear my mind and complete my press-up. I take a few nice slow breaths, still thinking of how I could've done so much more but getting to grips with the thought process of the system. Now we have the life diary, so before we do today's, take five minutes and relive yesterday's proud moment before you write down today's. So today's life diary is a proud moment entry. This entry may seem minuscule to some, but to me, it stood out, so this one day, I decide to go to a coffee shop for a well-deserved cappuccino, and as I enter, an old lady is trying to leave the shop, so I hold the door for her, she takes quite a while so when she says, "Thank you very much."

I reply, "No problem, anytime; would you like me to escort you to your car?"

She replied, "No, thank you," and went on.

Then I returned to the coffee shop, and the ladies that had been sitting with her said to me, "It's so nice to see good manners and respect; you really made our friend's day, thank you."

I said, "It's fine, anytime."

It was only after I had got my cappuccino and sat down that I started to think about what had just taken place. You see, good manners and people skills are something to be very proud of, and it made me smile - on our fridge at home, my five year old son has an award for cheerful greeting and good conversation. I think if you always try to give a little extra, your rewards will come, as my fridge proves. Next, as before, shower and breakfast (healthy breakfast optional).

WEEK ONE WEDNESDAY

6.00 am (tired)

Three pounds in my cup now clear my mind and breath and complete my push-up. Don't think about doing any more reps now; just follow the system. Next, as always, is my life diary, another proud moment in my life like yesterday. You must try to think about the previous proud moments you have written down as this is a very important part of the process. This one is about the birth of my son. To say the pregnancy and birth were stressful is an understatement but the courage shown by my wife during this process was next level. I feel proud because we had a lot of mountains to climb, but we climbed them together and ended up with a beautiful son who continues to make me the proudest dad ever..

Next is the shower, followed by a healthy breakfast.

WEEK ONE THURSDAY

6.00 am (tired but not surprised)

I'm starting to enjoy filling the cup now because I can see four pounds in my cup, and for some reason, that makes me feel positive; it might be that now I'm adding up in my mind that consistency creates results. So now, the breathing exercise I choose to do a four-second intake and a four-second exhale five times. I feel that's enough for me to get in my zone. I get my press-up done and go straight into my proud moment in my life. This moment for me is when I got my driver's licence; it gave me freedom and the ability to earn money which is of paramount importance to me, it may not seem much to everybody, but to me, it was a great accomplishment.

When I see some of my proudest moments written down, it makes me realise that I have accomplished and continue to accomplish many things in my life, and maybe sometimes, when I am feeling negative emotions reading these proud points could instigate positive energy production.

Shower and healthy breakfast.

WEEK ONE FRIDAY

6.00 am (feeling positive)

Five pounds in my cup now, and the funny thing is when I hear the sound of those pound coins hitting other pound coins, I actually feel positive in the knowledge that I have accomplished press-ups to equal those pound coins and gained from both. Now the breathing concentrates and clears my mind, and I'm ready for my push-up. I know now in my mind I am capable of so much more, and it fills me with positivity. I can see how the system puts you in a state of perpetual frustration because it does seem pointless at the beginning, but as you do the press-ups and add the pounds and remember the proud points, it all starts to make sense; you see you have to do system this way for it to work for you. You must always remember you are in this for the long term, and for that, it must be absolutely sustainable, and the only way it can be completely sustainable is by the tiny increments of both pennies and push-ups and backed up by a foundation of your own achievements in life. So on to my push-up, slow down, slow up, now, my life diary; when thinking about this entry, I am already thinking about my other four entries; the birth of my son, my driver's licence, my manners and social skills, my achievements with team sports and I actually feel proud of myself I do feel an increase in self-worth and a positive feeling for doing this system I just need to keep the consistency up. So my final proud point of the week is that although I am not a hugely confident person within myself, for me to write this book has taken a lot of courage and honesty from myself. The fact that I have has made me extremely proud. I have gone against what my mind was telling me and went with my heart; all too often, I am ruled by my mind, and I believe this in itself constrains me. I had to face my fear to unlock my true potential now. I am not saying this works for everybody but for me; I had to control my 'what if' mentality and put more into the 'I can' mentality. I have to back myself, and believe me anxiety, and low self-esteem makes this incredibly difficult to attain. And that's why I think this system will work; it constantly reminds you of your own self-worth and accomplishment via the life diary, and doing so actually forces you to be positive and have the ability to manufacture positivity through your own actions.

So to the shower and healthy breakfast, and that's week one done. As you can see, the following three weeks need to be completed in the same fashion, except the only differences are the content of the life diary and the amount of money that you put in your pot, and the number of push-ups or your chosen exercise you do every day so it may look something like this.

WEEK TWO

One pound in a pot (optional), two press-ups and the life diary subject matter are specific positive acts you have done in your life. shower and healthy breakfast.

WEEK THREE

One pound in pot three press up life diary subject matter is your future aspirations, what you want to achieve your goals shower, and healthy breakfast.

WEEK FOUR

One pound in a pot, four press-ups and the life diary subject matter is whatever you think is stopping you from attaining your goals shower and a healthy breakfast.

WEEK FIVE

One pound fifty in my pot, five press-ups and my life diary subject matter is how do I get through and defeat whatever it is that is stopping me from obtaining my goals.

So if you structure your system like this one, you will see that the realisation and remembrance of your own achievements are key; then the setting of goals is equally important, and the understanding of the things that may stop you attain your goals and putting in place solutions to deal with them you now have a structure by which you can improve physically, mentally and financially but it must be done with the tiny increments of pennies and push-ups.

WHY SO SMALL?

The reason the pennies and press-ups numbers are so small is to maintain consistency. If you control the increments with small numbers, the system will, in effect, force you into the mindset of challenging yourself to do more than you know you are capable of. It may sound pointless, but life rarely gives us this choice of mindset a lot of the time; it just gives us a mountain to climb, and a pair of flip flops to climb it in. The reason many of us do not stick to diets or the gym is because of this all-or-nothing mentality; it's just too extreme and hard to smash the gym or do a full-on diet or even save money. I believe this is because a lot of us do these things because we have to, not because we want to. I'm hoping that this system teaches people that health and well-being can be a part of your life on a daily basis if it is made almost harder not to do it because of the tiny increments of effort required to maintain the Brutal Mindset system.

Chapter 4: Life Diary

One way that helps you see and understand your problems better is writing them down. Be it with pen and paper, or on a notes app on your digital device. Mere mental acknowledgement of problems and issues will make you more anxious and worried. It will surely not enable you to think of the most effective, all-round solutions because if all your issues are just flying around your mind, there can be very little order to them. This makes you feel very out of control. As the life diary is written, this in itself brings a level of order that may bring you some peace. You may find a few connections within your writing if maybe one of your goals is to get further at your work yet one of your personality traits is low confidence you may be able to work on these better if in the visual form of the life diary you can see what you need to work on to achieve your goals and hopefully the manufacture of your own positive energy could play a part in attaining them.

It is very important that a problem be written next to a plausible solution, so that when you achieve it, you have an idea of what you had to do to get through that particular issue. If you keep writing all your mental experiences – both positive and negative – down, you can start to put together the necessary solutions to deal with them.

If you could have a visual reminder of how you overcame certain issues, one look at your diary whenever you may require it, may be beneficial. Also, you must fully understand the order of events regarding what needs to take place in order to deal with that problem.

For instance, if one of your issues is of a financial nature, say, a lack of money, then adjacent to this particular problem, you must write something like, "If I work a little extra or get another job for a little extra cash, or try to put a little bit more in my pot, after a certain length of time my money will increase, and my financial issues may improve.If I continue doing this consistently for a longer period of time, I will accumulate more. Or I can put two pounds a day in my penny jar, then after a certain amount of time, I would have this much extra cash.

"If I do all this together or separately but consistently for a while, I will continue to make more money, and thus alleviate some of the stress of having issues with money." Of course, it may not be as easy as this to simply come up with solutions for every issue. If finding solutions was that easy we would all be thriving despite our issues .

However, this is where journaling issues and solutions might help. Journaling these solutions is better because when you can visualise the situations, you can come up with a positive system to deal with the problems before they become issues.

By this I mean, there are usually many peripheral issues surrounding the main problem that needs sorting out, so when you can see all these issues they become a lot easier to deal with. So as with the financial issue, your need to have more money for whatever reason, it may have many reasons as to why you cannot make that money, you may already have more jobs or your outgoings are already high so it makes it hard to actually make more money. This system tries to solve this by building into you that consistency to add to your worth both physically mentally and financially but this takes time as the person with finance issues needs pounds not pennies. A big part of the system again is consistency.

The man or woman who needs more money must understand that it must be planned and stuck to because quick fixes are not part of the system. After one year, you will be inevitably better off financially but will really only be of major help after doing the system for years consistently.

This way of sorting problems out may seem far too incrementally small for you to deal with, but you must realise that this lesson here, if learned and executed correctly can support you consistently for serious amounts of time.

Also the one thing you have a major abundance of is time. Remember this. So using this method, making time work for you, that is the key.

We all too quickly can be brought down by negativity because we do not seem to have enough positive energy to outweigh the negativity, but just think how much more organised your mind would be once you make a habit of writing issues and potential solutions down, when having them compiled with you in written form, almost like a to-do list, almost like a grocery list. Also this writing habit encourages us to tackle one issue or many issues at a time, unlike what we do when our problems exist merely in our heads they seem to be of greater numbers. And for some reason, when you don't know their actual number, you seem to think they are in their thousands when in reality, they are few in number once you write these down.

We need to get away from burying our heads in the sand.

Let's just say that if you had been doing the penny and a push-up challenge for a year, where you put a pound in a jar every time you push up, you would safely have £365 at the end of the year and be a lot better at pushups with a better mindset with the use of your life diary as well.

You would realise that the fact that you have stuck to something for a set amount of time without fail and have reaped the rewards for that very little physical or mental outlay. It is proof that big changes for progression in life can start with tiny actions. The most value-adding factor to these small habits and tiny routines is consistency and faith in them.

This system may just change your mindset from dealing with problems when they occur to dealing with them before they do. You will experience a sense of relief and light-weightiness that happens when negativity and problems are not weighing people down.

The bonus to mental health from this system is that if you can imagine, it is not just money that you have saved in your jar, but self-confidence, self-worth and a sense of accomplishment. It may just increase these positive emotions to benefit yourself, it's quite amazing to think that a simple set of actions could have such positive and life-altering results, once again only if done consistently.

So let's say we are trying to address the things in life that are creating and holding negative energy. It is really up to you to determine what your cause of negative energy could be because, in the long run, the best way you will have for improving your life are the parts of your life that were once negative becoming positive and monitoring the parts of you from which negativity resides and hopefully controlling them.

For example, for some people, this negative energy could manifest itself as low self-esteem, depression, confidence issues in such situations, the person in question may have recently gone through a rough patch in their life where they may have issues with someone very close and beloved, or just that person's own demons becoming an issue, as a reaction to this the person may start doing certain negative activities to extremes. This could be drinking, drugs, sex and could be happening on a regular basis as a coping strategy for the negative emotions that person is experiencing it could and quite often does affect their body in a negative way because of the derogatory effect that most addictive substances have upon your mind and body.

Spending so much time in negative surroundings will eventually lead them spiralling into a bigger crisis where they may even lose their job or relationship, and that in itself can lead to an altogether darker scenario. This scenario may seem extreme but to some people living with mental health this is par for the course. They may develop serious health issues or may make them prone to bouts of depression. So what once was a problem that could have been easily tackled would become insurmountable.

Tapping in intellectually with your emotions and problems can avoid such a turn of events. So, again, the person with the fear of being crippled by loneliness can write

60

this valid concern in their list of problems in their life diary. Right next to it, they can add healthier options of how to avoid being lonely. They could get a new hobby and start taking evening or weekend classes for it, such as pottery, sculpting, carpentry, writing, or even joining a book club. Now, this may sound very basic, but positive social interaction is key to certain mental health issues.

They could go into gatherings related to this issue. They could make plans with friends to visit places like art museums or go on little picnics now and then. They could allot the evenings for essential work that buries their mind, such as deep cleaning the house, fixing things around their living space that they have been putting off. So in this way, not only will the person have an immediate partial solution to their problem, they will eventually learn to come to terms with being alone and not feeling lonely about it. They would work on their fear and overcome it. Using the system forces you to become more consistent and thus in time you could maybe deal with situations in a more level way.

So as we can see, another big upside is becoming more positive with time. So, for me, as an example, I permanently worry about other people's opinions of me. Now, most people would not really care about what other people think about because a lot of people just live their life. However, what my particular type of mental health does to me is the flip-side of this scenario altogether. Quite unfortunately, I do not particularly care about myself at all, especially when it comes to being constantly bothered and worried about what other people think of me.

What ends up happening in some situations is, you give all and the best of yourself to someone who is not important. While it is great to be good to everyone, the downside is that you are still mentally struggling and have nothing left in the tank for the people who are special to you and are most deserving of your love, energy and time. I think a certain portion of my mental health has me trying to justify my actions to myself even though I know this is a toxic habit in me. This is because of how much I try to give to everything I do, not leaving much even for myself.

Hence, I need to swap this habit and mental state, just give what is needed to be given, and I don't have to give everything and concentrate more on the people who give to me and give more to them. This realisation can really help anybody whose mental health manifests itself in this way. The way in which this particular part of mental wellness works is possibly one of the worst because many people are damaged by this active consciousness of being a people-pleaser because it is such hard work both physically and mentally.

I mean some people have had major negative incidents occur in their lives, either mentally, physically or both, become very susceptible to this master-servant personality trait. I believe many people have this issue simply because they didn't know how to train their minds and heart in the correct way. They did not teach themselves to derive a feeling of self-worth and self-love out of their accomplishments and good traits. This leaves them in a constant yearning for validation and external love. If you live your life never reminding yourself of your true self-worth, then as are most things that are left unpracticed.

Chapter 5: Treat Yourself Like A Business

This section is all about how you treat and feel about yourself; you cannot start this health and well-being journey without an understanding that you need to respect and love and know yourself before you can improve yourself. You need to know you are capable of the journey to reap the rewards of the destination. I will say this, whatever your situation, you spend no longer time on your own than when you are trying to work out what's lacking in your life. You will soon find out very quickly that wondering why you don't have certain things you want is a very negative mindset, yet the planning and attainment of these things you think you don't have requires a very positive mindset. Like a business, you must invest plenty of time in yourself to be able to plan and reach your own personal goals.

We waste far too much time wondering why when all we need to think is when, when you decide to take positive steps to attain your goals, you reap the benefits in every facet of your life. To do this effectively, though, you must realise your own full potential; you need to know what you are capable of in order to be confident enough to achieve your goals.

You must fuel your business with the correct mindset; you must live a certain way to reap the rewards of your own potential, and this way is one of healthy nutrition, a positive mindset, and an unnerving positive attitude towards whatever it is that you need to achieve.

So for me, my biggest issue is self-worth, so I need to be successful at what I do to show everyone I am worthy. Now a lot of people may say that I need to fix this "need to be successful" issue first; well, I decided to use my issue for my own personal gain. I started by writing down what I was good at and what I enjoyed doing so I'm good at lifting weights, I'm good at talking to people, I like looking fit and healthy, so instead of becoming a powerlifting social worker who wears tight pants with a false tan, I decided to try and mix my interests and abilities together to put together a system to not only assist in giving people a comfortable option to keeping fit and some basic nutrition choices, but also chance to maybe deal with certain issues that can affect people in life primarily mental health issues. The only reason I added the mental health portion to my system was because of the knowledge I have of my struggles with mental health and looking around at various other health and well-being systems, they seem to stick to health and nutrition only, I think a lot of people are a bit daunted by mental health issues, but I think to get the most out of a truly healthy lifestyle your mental health must take centre stage.

So how do I use my mental health in a positive way? Well, the way I do it is quite simple. I invest my time in things that will make my life a positive and worthwhile place for me to be in, so for instance, for me, consistency is my key. I try to do certain things consistently every day.

I will get up and do my Brutal Mindset system with a healthy breakfast. Doing these few things in the morning gives me the positivity and energy to achieve my daily goals with the correct mindset.

Some days I wake up with full-on negativity, so I don't want the Brutal Mindset system at all. I don't want any positivity at all, so what do I do then? Well, what I do is the exact polar opposite of what my mental health is telling me to, so I read my life diary do you press-ups put the pound in the cup, have a healthy breakfast, don't be negative to other people do go to work and believe me it's a lot harder to do than writing, but when you consistently deal with it this way at some point with the assistance of brutal mindset you can begin to feel lighter and more positive on your negative days.

Chapter 6: What Do You Want?

Never lose sight of your goal and map out your journey step by step; follow this and unlock your full potential.

Consistency is the key.

Chapter 7: Mental Health: A Destination, a Process

Now, you must understand that this illness is all-consuming and in itself has the capability of destroying the most stable people. Mental health is a complete reshaping of thinking and regulating your feelings and behaviour. Most people experience a disturbance in their mental functioning at least once. A change in your pattern of thinking, feeling, or behaving can cause stress or disrupt a person's ability to function. If you notice a change in yourself if you struggle with maintaining personal or family relationships, functioning in social settings, performing at your workplace, or learning at a level expected for your age and intelligence. You may also observe the change if you participate in other essential activities. Sometimes, cultural norms and social expectations can define mental health disorders. There are no set standards for measuring whether a person is expected or needs a consistent check-up. You must be the gauge, you must not be apprehensive to seek help for mental health issues.

Every mental health condition has its own indications and symptoms. Professional help is needed if you experience marked personality changes or sleeping patterns, withdrawal from your social circle and activities, unusual and overthinking, excessive anxiety and extreme mood swings.

Most people with mental health conditions consider these symptoms a normal part of life to run away from treatment. Primarily people do not seek help out of shame or fear. It is of utmost importance to find a professional familiar with your culture and social context relevant to your experiences and story.

You see, some people with no affliction have a predisposed idea of what a person with mental health issues looks and acts like. So a joker-ish trembling, crouched-over maniac, sweating profusely and talking in tongues is a misrepresentation of what a person with mental health issues is like. Exceptions, of course, are always there. Still, I am here having total sympathy with normally functioning, working people trying to manage this awful illness whilst trying to live everyday life.

Invisible health conditions are the most common among people. A lot of people have hidden disabilities, including physical conditions like hearing loss or neurological disorders or mental health conditions like anxiety, ADHD, post-traumatic stress disorder or an eating and sleeping disorder. People with invisible mental health conditions look fine from outside, but the inner reality tells a different story. Despite the age, we still live in an era where judging a book by its cover is very common. Our opinions have resulted from the way we look. The social media that controls us is an illusion of perfection we see through scrolling, like the endless happy moments of selfies from friends and strangers, captured at their best which keeps us in a delusion about how perfect their lives must be.

The small perfect moments we see leave us envious, creating a whole narrative for that person based on those moments without realising what troubles they might have had to face to reach that point. Many people on the outside look fine every day, even good looking individuals, who on the outside are very confident, the life and soul of the party, a great show for the crowd, because in all reality when the lights go out and nobody is looking, there is no need for the false-positive facade to continue. It is at these times that mental health issues can become most dangerous.

With the rise of social media as a new normal, we have become so occupied with looking 'happy and healthy' that we have forgotten the importance of mental health regardless of how people perceive us to be. We are more concerned about whether we look fine from the outside than actually feeling it. It has become difficult for people with invisible conditions to express or get help for their afflictions. There is more to mental health than what is perceived by the eye. The most important thing is paying attention to how people feel, being there for them when they need help, and giving them a safe place to let out their emotions.

71

Then there is the most common question that people ask and is inevitably answered. It usually goes like this "you look a bit down are you OK" answer "yes I'm ok" and that's that. You are left there to either dig a little deeper or leave it alone if you feel someone you know is struggling with mental health dig a bit deeper. They may be able to offload some weight which helps when the negatives, which are again starting to break down your defences with consummate ease, start to return. If you often catch yourself in negative self-talk, try to emphasise positive self-talk. Positive self-talk can lead you out of stress, mainly depending on your personality. This is why having daily increments of positive energy produced by yourself is imperative.

MY MUM'S ROLE

Mums are an amazing breed in nature. They give birth to their children and, from that point, play the most significant role in their children's lives. I am sharing my opinion here and nothing more. My own experiences are heavily affected by my relationship with my mum. It could be your dad or anyone you truly care for, when mums do this momentous task of raising children with little moaning, this on its own has a major part to play when trying to understand mental health in women. Social and economic factors can expose women to poor mental health conditions compared to men.

Women can experience issues such as depression and anxiety. There can be numerous reasons as to why they develop, and some factors affect women more. For instance, women are the nurturers who selflessly care for everyone while often neglecting their own needs. Domestic abuse can have a long term impact on mental health, post-traumatic stress disorder being the most common. Because the terms of domestic abuse are so varied, a woman could be in a very controlling relationship, and that would be enough to instigate mental health issues.

Women often find it hard to share their emotions, and as a result, tend to internalise them. leading to problems such as depression, eating disorders, insomnia, and self-harm.

Women already have a massive weight of responsibility to deal with before they can start to deal with any other issues that they may have in their life. Their life is one of caring for their family and partner. Even a minor fracture in a woman's mind, with the intense levels of responsibility, can create an extremely dangerous scenario that can have deadly repercussions if not dealt with, mental health should never be neglected. The psychological patterns of distress and disorders among women are different as compared to men. They have substantial power to internalise emotions.

Women predominate in the rates of common mental disorders. The differences between genders is also due to

73

clinical features, onset symptoms, social adjustments and long-term outcomes of severe mental disorders.

MY MUM

I knew I loved to help my mum at a young age but could not really define it, I just liked to see her smile. It was so much more than just washing up. You see, my mum was a very moralistic, ethically driven person. She taught me various things in life, and above all, she taught me how to stay solid on the right path. Wherever you go in life, there are some lessons that stay with you forever. The same was the case with me; I remember my mum taught me that whatever you do in life, there is always a right way and a wrong way of doing it.

To explain it further, let us look at a situation where you go shopping, and when you get to the counter, you pay for your goods and leave. Sounds right? Yes, but the other way is to get that very same amount of goods, yet when you get to the counter, you just walk out without paying for it. It's that simple, and that's how I was brought up and exactly how I tried to live all my life.

I understood why she was tired sometimes and helped out as much as possible but with three children and a full-time job, that in itself is a big mountain to climb.

Women who are managing their jobs and home simultaneously are the real heroes. Working and balancing home-life is a major challenge. Organisations should take a step forward by promoting work-life balance and flexible work arrangements to avoid a setback in reaching gender equality in the workplace. Also, the effect of paid and unpaid work that women deal with daily increases women's mental load.

You should never underestimate or take for granted the amount of pressure put on a woman to be a mother. Mothers play a vital role in building a home and making a family. The bonding you build over time is precious and irreplaceable. It is something that should be realised for what it is. Maybe sometimes, take a minute and hug your mum. Imagine when you will be at their stage, show the gratitude and love you would expect in the future. It is easier said than done because we as children are so indulged in our lives that we forget to have those precious moments with family. The family time you spend with your siblings and parents should never be taken for granted. The moment you have with them is all you will ever need in your hard times. As a daughter, son, husband, just whisper some words of kindness or a simple 'thank you'; believe me, it's what they deserve.

Chapter 8: The Complexity of a Mind With Mental Health

Sometimes I wish my mental health could take a form that mirrors its actual characteristics so that I could show others how terrible a foe it is. This physical form of mental health would be so horrifying that, I am sure, the necessary authorities would take more action. The problem is, yet again, one of the most prolific killers has no face. Our mental and physical health is closely interlinked. People with long-term physical health conditions are likely to experience mental health problems like anxiety and depression.

Mental ill-health is unavoidable, and there is support and certified ways to help yourself. The long-term conditions are not cured completely but can be managed by medication, also termed chronic conditions like epilepsy, asthma, arthritis etc. At some point in your life, you can be affected by such conditions that can adversely affect your relationships, ability to focus and mental health. Such physical conditions can result in low self-esteem, stigma, social isolation and anxiety. You might feel stressed, tired, depressed especially when dealing with your mental health.

All the things mentioned earlier will most likely develop mental health problems like anxiety and depression. Mental health problems can make it difficult to cope with your life in general.

Nowadays, we throw the word depression around as if it's something very common. Be it a bad day or something that stops you from living life, we often label it as depression.

How does this depression start? It slowly begins and takes over a person's life. Small, unnoticeable things change at first, leading to more considerable changes. Then you reach the point where the black cloud is over your head. If I describe the state of my depression, it is hard to put it into words. Depression is when things change around you, or maybe they don't change; it is your perspective of looking at things that need to change. It is a state where you feel so low that the things that once made you happy do not hold the same emotions. You keep wondering what makes you different from others, you force yourself to get out of bed every day, and you drag yourself around each day.

The efforts you make to push yourself for everything are tremendous. You will hear most people saying depression is cured by expressing , but how do you talk about something so hard to understand yourself? Depression is not a choice but a reaction to life that you never imagined to be yours. Depression is a reaction to stress and the inability to change your situation. Depression consumes you, and it is a deep sadness and regret. For any person reading this that can relate to any of the above things, it is high time to seek help. Depression can be helped, the early stages of it can be eased by doing things you enjoy and that improve you as a person like painting, playing with your kids and going out for a walk attaining what you require in life.

The first step to betterment is that there should be acceptance. Accept that depression is a part of your life. Own up to it for yourself and learn to be okay with it. Secondly, allow yourself to be patient and give yourself some time to heal. It does not happen overnight, and it slowly gets better with time. Lastly, as impossible as it seems to be, you should get help from external resources. Getting help does not mean they will cast a magic spell, and everything will be alright. It is like they will support you no matter how hard things get; they make you see the light even if there is no light at the end of the tunnel. Most people have depression, and they come out of it stronger than ever before. With a brutal mindset, I hope to make you physically and financially, and mentally strong enough to deal with your issues.

One of the most common and effective methods is Cognitive Behavioural Therapy (CBT), which can help change your mindset and feel better about things. It can help regulate your pain and understand the underlying reason for mental health problems.

It is challenging to understand mental health purely because every symptom and feeling by anyone with a semblance of mental health is subjective unless you have the capability to connect with that emotion. People often assume that depression is a single, uniform feeling – deep sadness and loss of interest in daily activities that most people enjoy doing the most. Depression is complicated to define as it varies from person to person. It varies mainly because depression is based on people's psychological symptoms and behaviours, not from physical wounds.

Often when depression is diagnosed, we rely on symptoms defined by other people. We have to trust doctors to analyse and probe their symptoms deeply. We have to understand that the feelings of the people suffering from depression vary from people who do not.

Many countries now screen for depression in the general public, not just a small group of people who are under therapy. Secondly, the questionnaires and interviews are conducted that treat depression as a condition that can occur at any level at any time. Lastly, other statistical tools can help us understand how symptoms are related to one another.

If you find it difficult to understand why someone would feel that driving their car to a desolate area, placing a pipe from the exhaust through the window and slowly slipping away is the answer.. Helping someone with depression can be challenging. It takes your unlimited understanding to help them to keep striving harder to be positive. If someone very near to you is depressed or going through any mental illness, you might be experiencing a number of difficult emotions, including frustration, anger, helplessness, and sadness. The feelings are normal, and not easy to deal with. It can become overwhelming, but once again, consistency is the key.

Your companionship can be essential to your beloved's recovery as you can help them cope with symptoms, help them overcome powerful negative thoughts, and regain their energy and optimism. On the way to helping your beloved climb to the top of the mountain, always remember the journey is worth it. It is essential to provide full support to your loved ones, and you can only do that when you are totally invested in the system. It would help if you never underestimated how powerful depression is as it drains a person's energy, motivation and optimism. You just cannot expect them to feel as good as you feel about a certain thing. They cannot just snap out of it by force of will.

The symptoms of mental illness and depression are personal. It makes it challenging to connect emotionally with anyone, even with the people they love. It makes them emotionally unavailable. Also, most of the time, people with severe depression lash out in anger. The key to dealing with such a situation is that it is their depression talking, not their loved ones.

BE HONEST

Getting away with depression by closing your eyes is not a workable solution. Hiding away from the problem does not help anyone if it involves making excuses to cover up the problem. It keeps the depressed person away from seeking treatment. It would help if you remembered that your beloved one is not lazy or unmotivated; it's just mental health is a strong adversary. You must feel positive when you think about doing things that can help them. Down the line, one important thing to remember is that you cannot fix someone else's depression, you can help them lessen the weight by understanding. It is a terrible feeling to see them suffer; you cannot take away their pain as much as you want to. You might feel guilty for not being able to help them out completely. You can offer them love and support, and recovery is mostly in the hands of the depressed person but when they experience your unreserved understanding believe me it makes a difference.

How can you recognise depression symptoms in your loved ones? It is very crucial to understand the symptoms of depression. It might start with something as small as sleeping less than usual. You might notice symptoms in your depressed ones before they do, and your kindness can help them feel encouraged to seek help. If you observe the following symptoms, they need help:

- If they have lost interest in work, hobbies and other activities they liked doing or they withdraw from their friends and family.

- They express a negative outlook on life. They quickly lose temper, get mood swings and feel hopeless and helpless.

- They frequently complain about their physical pain like back pain, stomach problems, and feeling drained out.

- They sleep less or more than usual. They have become forgetful, disorganised and indecisive.

- They have an eating disorder.

Sometimes, it becomes difficult to see our loved ones suffering when we love them so much. It is a feeling of helplessness when you want to help, but you cannot find the right way to do so. It is hard to know what to say as you might fear that if you mention your concerns, the other person will get angry or feel insulted. If you are unsure where to start, remember a few things that can help you, like being a compassionate listener because it is much more important than giving advice. Sometimes we do not need a solution, and we need someone who can listen to us and make us feel at home. Encourage the person to vent out and let their emotions speak without the fear of being judged.

One more important thing is to remember that do not expect a solution from a single conversation. Depressed people often isolate themselves as you might need to express your concerns and be willing to listen over and over again. Finding the right words is always the hardest part. You can practice by saying, *'I have been feeling concerned about you'* or *'recently I have noticed some differences and wondered what you are doing.'* Being too concerned can also make the person feel irritated. Show your genuine concerns and give them some personal space to let the emotions pass through them.

Your kindness is your greatest strength, so it is advisable to keep a stronghold on this quality while dealing with depressed loved ones. You can say things like those mentioned below to help them feel better.

'You are not alone, and we can go through this together.'

'Your feelings are valid; whatever you are feeling is justified.'

'It might be hard to believe right now, but your feelings will change.'

'Please let me know what I can do for you.'

'I might not be able to understand exactly how you feel, but you are not alone, and I care about you.'

'You matter.'

'When you feel like giving up, remind yourself that it is just one more day, hour or minute.'

Avoid saying the following things:

'You are overthinking.'

'Try to look on the brighter side.'

'You feel negative all the time,'

'You should feel better now.'

I, you see, have been to that world and to some level, I live there forever bound to live my life with mental health issues, but also because of my unique relationship with the beast have created a system by which my life can have normality to some degree. I have been through this rollercoaster ride, it was not easy, but I came out of it. My depression did not take a consistent hold of my life. I was motivated to change how I felt, which is the most crucial part of getting treated. Once you gather your inner strength and make your willpower strong, there is nothing to hold you back from gaining consistency in your life again. You can do this!

Nutrition and Exercise Use Your Conscience to Benefit Your Well-Being

This part of the book is very important as it brings into the forefront of mental health the importance of conscience. My conscience is a voice I use to empower me with my own mental and physical goals I have achieved, every tiny exercise I complete to every piece of healthy food I eat adds to my little voice, my conscience that gives me a reason to carry on with my positive actions. I use my conscience as my own personal positive storage system. It can make me stay positive through the amount of positive actions I complete, this is because when I am doing these positive actions daily for me to start becoming negative means I give all my positives away to some extent. This conflict of interests within me makes me highlight the positive against the negative and with me doing this my sense of achievement comes into the forefront of my mind. I start asking myself why I am feeling so negative when I have weeks and weeks of positive actions in my conscience bank. I soon start to think the amount of tiny increments of positivity can add up to help me fight the beast when it comes. With this in mind I sought to find a major link between nutrition exercise and mental positivity so firstly we shall delve into the intense and intricate world of the mind and its connection to emotions through various chemical releases in the body that can have major effects on your mental health. Emotions are the starting point for most of my issues however the size of one emotion in comparison to another emotion is the mixing pot that can become very dangerous if not monitored very closely, The outcome if this can be either very positive or

85

very negative these are the peaks and troughs that I spoke of earlier hopefully with a positive system in place you can attain consistency between your peaks and troughs to a more stable chain mindset.

The amount of certain chemicals your body releases can have a massive effect on your mental health, the amount of these chemicals that get released during different situations can vary massively from person to person these chemicals can have drastic effects on your mental health during specific scenarios I am only writing these pieces of information down because at the very least if you could maybe relate some of your dark feelings to the fact that it is your body releasing certain chemicals and not you becoming engulfed by the beast, you may hope at least realise that it's not all you it's actually something that can be explained and treated. The next bit is science so just try to get the main gist of what I am trying to put forward this bit to me was the most beneficial because it gave me hope that I wasn't mad.

The four primary positive chemicals are dopamine, oxytocin, serotonin, and endorphins.

Dopamine:

This is a chemical messenger that your nervous system uses to send messages between nerve cells. Dopamine plays a role in how we feel pleasure and plays a big part in how we think and plan, also to strive, focus and find things interesting. You probably won't notice it until something goes wrong. Too much or too little can have an effect and lead to health issues.

Too much dopamine can have these effects: high libido, anxiety, stress, improved ability to focus and learn, difficulty sleeping as you can see consistently inconsistent.

Too little dopamine can have these effects chronic back pain, low libido, weight fluctuations, fatigue, attention difficulties, to name a few

Functions dopamine affects:

Motivation, heart rate, blood vessel function, kidney function, lactation, sleep mood, attention, control of nausea and vomiting, pain processing, movement.

Foods that boost dopamine are as follows: bananas, almonds, strawberries, pineapple, green tea, pumpkin seeds, raw chocolate, omega 3 rich fish salmon, Mackerel etc. also chicken, beef, and turkey.

Dopamine boosting activities:

A balanced diet of protein, fats, carbohydrates, vitamins and minerals.

Enough rest and sleep.

Exercising.

Listening to music.

Get outdoors into the sunlight.

Dopamine helps with motivation which as we know can take a major hit when mental health is involved just know that there may be other things playing a part in your mental health as well. **Oxytocin:**

A hormone and neurotransmitter associated with empathy, trust, sexual activity, and relationship building. It's called the love drug because levels of oxytocin rise when hugging and during orgasm. In women it is released in high doses during labour and has a big role to play in the whole birth cycle.

The results of having too much oxytocin in your system are unclear at present. But prostate issues have been linked.

But having too little oxytocin in your system has been linked to autism and autistic spectrum disorders with poor social functioning as well, also low levels of empathy.

Functions oxytocin affects:

Oxytocin affects both positive and negative emotions but it's main use is in the pregnancy and birth cycles as it stimulates the contractions during labour it also has a major effect on relationship's by the way it affects social bonding which is why it's called the love drug but also has the negative side as well by making us connect with people like ourselves yet not so with people who are different to us.

Foods that boost oxytocin:

Fatty fish mushrooms, tomatoes, peppers, spinach, avocados, vitamins A and D magnesium and dietary fats.

Oxytocin boosting activities

Yoga

Massage

Meaningful conversation

Telling people your positive feelings about them

Meditation

Spending time with your friends.

Oxytocin is an amazing hormone that really connects you socially and has many emotional traits that are both positive and negative. The fact that it is produced through social interactions means that with regards to mental health it could play a big part in the helping of certain issues. It would be quite interesting to see if there are any links between postnatal depression and any other pregnancy type mental health issues.

Serotonin:

Serotonin is found mainly in the blood and digestive system and central nervous system; it helps regulate behaviour, attention and body temperature. It also plays a part in the regulation of the digestive process, blood flow and breathing. Also mood, cognition, reward, memory.to name a few.

Results of too much serotonin:

Shivering

Diarrhoea

Muscle rigidity

Fever

Seizures

Results of too little serotonin:

Feelings of sadness

Hopelessness

Chronic Fatigue

Anger

Suicidal tendencies

Sleep trouble

Functions Serotonin affects

Mood

Emotions

Appetite

Digestion

Foods that boost serotonin:

Salmon

Nuts

Milk and cheese

Tofu

Pineapple

Eggs

Bananas

Spinach

Tomatoes

Serotonin boosting activities:

Good nutrition

Meditation

Attaining goals

Regular exercise

Spend time in nature walking in visually stunning surroundings

Serotonin is very important in the body as it is a mood stabiliser and also a sleep stabiliser. An imbalance of serotonin can lead to anxiety, panic ,obsessive compulsive behaviour, and researchers believe it could lead to depression.

Endorphins:

Endorphins are the body's natural painkillers. They are released to counter pain and stress and also give us feelings of euphoria. Endorphins trigger a positive feeling throughout the body when the completion of certain physical activities are achieved .Also the addictive traits of endorphins make it quite dangerous when mixed with negative mental health issues. Some doctors have related the feel good emotion and reward portion of endorphins to both exercise and drug addiction. But saying this physical activity produces endorphins which in turn improves rest and can reduce some mental health symptoms. Endorphin deficiency can result in a lot of negative issues such as depression and low pleasure amounts in life. Also headaches and constant pain, major cravings for sugar alcohol etc. so really endorphins play a big role in positive mental health.

Foods that improve endorphin production:

Strawberries

Oranges

Grapes

Nuts and seeds

Eggs

Dark chocolate

Brown rice

Bananas

Activities to produce more endorphins:

Light exercise

Massage

Sexual intercourse

Having a good laugh with friends

Acupuncture

You see endorphins are extremely important with regards to mental health, but they can be both positive and negative with regards to mental health states as everything they have is not monitored accordingly.

I hope from this brief explanation and a glimpse of the different chemicals that affect your mood, you can see that they play a crucial role within the mental health spectrum. With the brutal mindset system in place and good nutrition and exercise done consistently you as a person with or without mental health issues can gain positivity from this book.

I really just made this system to try and push positivity both for people with mental health issues and without, for anybody finding living life difficult and finding it hard to accomplish goals just take what you can from this book, and I hope it somehow gets you to realise that you are the key and you have the ability to succeed at anything you put your head and your heart to.

If you take anything from this book take this.

YOU ARE THE KEY NEVER FORGET THIS.